Late Love

Late Love

Poems by

Paula Goldman

Cover design by Shay Culligan
Photograph by Meredith W. Watts, "For Good" Photography

ISBN: 978-1-950462-67-4

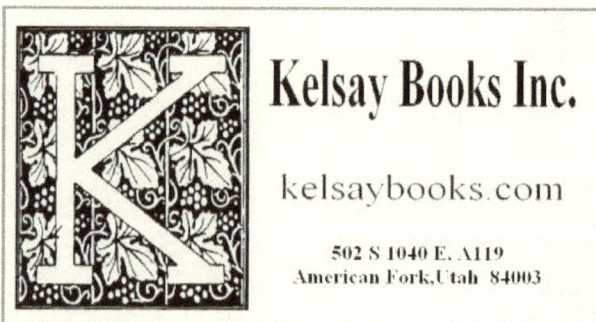

Kelsay Books Inc.

kelsaybooks.com

502 S 1040 E. A119
American Fork, Utah 84003

To Allan, thanks for the precious years.

Acknowledgments

Grateful acknowledgment is made to the editors and publisher of the following anthologies and periodicals in which these poems were first published.

American Writers Review 2019: "I am Beautiful"
American Writers Review Summer 2018: "The Handkerchief"
Bayou: "Egypt"
North American Review: "If Dickinson Had a Husband"
    finalist for the James Hearst Poetry Prize.
Rattle: "Bonnard's Wife's Ashes"
Prairie Schooner: "Portrait", "Wading"
Poetic Voices Without Borders, edited by Robert L. Giron:
    "Givenchy Lavender"
Visions International: "The Odalisque"
River Oak Review: "No More Arguments"
Slant: "Passage"
The Comstock Review: "Losing"
Slant: "The Girl in the Stone Creek Coffee Shop"
Quill and Parchment: "Now that we are leaving"
Passager: "Late Inamorato"
The Briar Cliff Review: "The Prayer of the Bone"
Cream City Review: "Praise the Manna and Pass the Ammunition"
5AM: "So I Go Shopping"
Ekphrasis: "As He Painted" "A Red Dachshund"
Oyez Review: "Thorns", "The Chicken"
Briar Cliff Review: "There are Rooms"
ARLIJO.COM: "As We Say Goodbye" Nominated for a Pushcart
    Award and "Mirror, Mirror."
The Journal of Poetry Center San José : "The Return"
Manhattanville Review: "Van Gogh's Prayer"
Calyx: "Amsterdam"
Dash: "A Bed of Scarves", "You Drew a Blank"
American Writers Review: "The Handkerchief"
Hawaii Pacific Review: "Life's Not a Novel"
Ekphrasis: "Discards"
Hawaii Pacific Review: "Golden Autumn"
The Awakenings Review: "When the Light Changed"

Much appreciation goes to Mark Cox, the late AV Christie, Sara Talpos, Renee Wolfson, Allan Goldman, MD, Mickey Hoffman, Katharine Mallin, Richard A Frank, MD, for their careful readings of the poems and to Rick Jackson for his continuing inspiration. And special thanks to Derek Schanz for all his kindness and work on the manuscript.

Contents

Section III

Section IV

Section I

If Dickinson had a Husband

I give you my poems to mail—
Dear Husband.
Later, you call to say
how sorry you are, throwing
in your briefcase first, leaving
the poems on top of the car
before driving off.

I walk to the kitchen window,
unraveling the phone cord
when I see them in the wind—

winged white sheets,
they sail from the brown envelope,
splitting apart like a milkweed pod—
the seeds flying far, far
over the avenue.

People jog,
push baby carriages,
walk their dogs—
stop and pick them up.
They read sestinas, villanelles, sonnets—
everyone reading my poems.

"Of course," I say and hang up.

A Bed of Scarves

Scarves thrown on the bed, a blend
 of black velvet and red roses, orange velvet appliqué,
  flowered calla lily chiffons, ruffled satins,
   Japanese waterfalls and bridges,

Scarves like those shirts Gatsby tossed
 ecstatically to show Daisy how far he'd come in
  this world from "Jimmy" Gatz, so many shirts he flew
   about the room, tears came to her eyes.

A scarf on Isadora Duncan's
 neck while she was driving a convertible in Nice, France
  caught in the open-poked wheels and rear axle,
   breaking her neck. Why does the beauty

of the world come to haunt me?
 Scarves covering a queen size bed, some queen, a butcher's
  daughter, above the butcher shop, where dead chickens
   dressed the window and cows' heads hung on hooks.

Scarves Mother wore on her head,
 babushkas. Material, matter, Mother. Her blood-stained
  aprons stank at the end of the day, as she did,
   the floor scrubbed daily, the butcher blocks.

Scarves I haul from the closet,
 floating over the bed won't console me anymore,
  a cry from for that lady unsexed. "Out, damn spot, I say,"
   repugnant odors, sights won't relent.

"I am Beautiful"

plaster 1882 by Auguste Rodin (1840-1917)

Was she flung, as if in a ball of flesh,
by a breath of wind into his torso?
Rodin had made them separately for
the Gates of Hell, but here, they are so
together they cannot be torn apart, his hand
grasps her kneecap. One arm surrounds
her buttock. The other holds her neck.
His back is arched to keep her steady.
Drawn as the sea is drawn to the beach;
they stand anchored; there is no tide out.
How I felt this way when we were first
together, upraised. I could not have been
more beautiful in anyone's eyes. But this
is art, not life where one separates
from the adored by whatever life brings,
its cargo of familiarities. In this instant
these two are one unit, Rodin's name signed
on the man's inside thigh, as if to say
"my thigh, I hold you against me forever."
I cannot fly from this image, now in bronze.
Time stops as I have, joined to our ardor.

The Human Heart

When I thumb the cool hollow
of her back, trace the curve
of her oval head, finger
the slight bumps of breasts, and below
where her folded arms rest, I know
what Freud must have felt
each morning, stroking
the antiquities on his desk,
what touch meant to him, helpmate
to the eye, abandoned by colleagues
and friends, reaching
into his own teeming
mind where both the goddess
and baboon reside, finding
what the human heart cannot deny,
wanting more than the *ordinary*
unhappiness of everyday
life, he so aptly described.
Failed heart, we were never
thine or *thine*. Who was that blond
woman on your arm? And the statue
stares and says, *What has happened to you?*

The Future

       We walked in the moment
Open to the alterable
Sea, keeping our ears to the surf.
~

       Wore your torn spotted sunhat,
The way you hold onto everything
And I give away, I give way.
~

       Believer in weather
Forecasts as devout pagans
Read animal entrails

As destiny, it's going to rain today.

The Return

Geese honk like horns on Model T's
in a black and white movie, scattering
chickens on a dusty street.

Daffodils spiral out of soil beds
like silly girls slipping out of old jeans
into prom dresses.

Lightning sparks rain instead of snow.
Soon my roses overturn brick-
weighted cones.

Who moved the stone, as heavy
as my heart, this winter,
and how far?

Evolution

You come home from your Marathon
like a soldier limping from a wound—
your Achilles' heel smarts. Your disc
worn out. You put down your shield,
your spear, your helmet still hanging
from your tanned arm. I take you
in my arms and we begin
the day to day battle, the terrible
grinding of years, taxes to Caesar, tuition
bondage, roof repairs, in care of . . . .
I still love you. *What are days for?*

"I Hate Vronsky!"

Sometimes she did not know what she feared, what she desired: ...
—Anna Karenina, Leo Tolstoy

I hate Vronsky! I love Vronsky!
I'm sick of Anna's longing. What if
he cracks his knuckles, same
as Karenin, her detested husband?
Why do we always read for news
of Anna and Vronsky, and not
Kitty and Levin, who share the married
harvests? And what of the lover
who's never there to shovel us
out of snowdrifts, drifts over
the vast steppes of Russia? No one
can see so far over these steppes:
these Oblonsky's Scherbatskaya's,
Tverskaya's. Where is the day to day
living? Does Vronsky snore? Does he leave
socks on the floor? Does he wear socks?
Who can live headily with the onslaught
 of the predictable? Anna jumps
before an oncoming train. So much
for ribbons and bows and Vronsky.

Boating

after Gabriele Münter's painting, 1910

He's standing in the boat.
She's rowing the boat.
Her back is to the viewer.
A storm is coming.
A black dog is jumping out,
A little boy with his hand
Between his tight thighs
Sits beside a woman
Wearing a large red hat.
The jagged mountains are deep blue.
The water is black blue.
The clouds are hanging darkly.
People stare blankly
From blue dots eyes.
It is a menacing painting.
There is no vanishing point.
Flat planes of color.
The standing man is Kandinsky,
Münter's teacher and lover.
She went in her own direction.
So did he, war and a wife.
Who's in charge?
The red mad gunwales
Of this boat are hotter
Than the heavy hats
Of the two women.
Is she heading into the storm?
Is she coming back to shore?

Reckoning

Like a ship floating
into mist, yet I'm told
if I can keep a *scrupulous*

account of my direction,
my speed, calculating
as decades pass,

eventually I'll deduce
my position. Sounds simple, but
take this street beyond

the bay window, it's barren
and gray, its borders
of parallel trees, lifeless,

and stingy. The only distinct
landmarks: my heartbeat
and a homing pigeon blown off

by electrical storms
It used to be a straight shot
to your office parking lot

from our house. But since
you've left town, husband,
I stumble from bed to bathroom,

the sweet wake of your after-
smoothed and gone. I'm in no
mood for marriage or morning.

The honeybee flies by the sun,
But most songbirds can't
learn new songs. When you

go away, I must master
cartography, when you return,
I think we're both mistakes

in the floor plan.

Passage

Think of a person as a passage...
—*John Koethe*

I looked hard, near and far
        as Omaha to see what you drew
    from Mont Ste-Victoire. Bored

with greenery, I squinted
        to see the cone, sphere, and cylinders,
    you revered, the mountain

risen like an iceberg.
        "Father of us all," Picasso said,
    but you could bear neither

touch nor praise. Your apples
        glow like pool balls, the cue forever
    rolled to the rails. Prickly,

easily enraged, nicknamed
        early in school *l'écorché*—the flayed one—
    afraid that people might get

their hooks into you. But
        with your friends, Zola and Baille, you roamed
    the countryside, swam,

transposing them on canvas
        to classical bathers, on the grass,
    beside streams, wading. Why

do I always chafe
        among people, wanting a separate
    place, then feel turned away?

24

Whatever happened
    to the unspoiled openness of clear
  summer days, white sands, safe

tides, wide lawns, lying down
    wide-eyed? Side by side, bikinied girls
  and briefed guys, stroking backs,

legs, arms, our sweat scented
    with pineapple, coconut, lime? But
  you, Cézanne, were fearful—

of women, especially.
    You painted a mountain, the same mountain
  60 times, like a woman

you were faithful to,
    but could never embrace, the painted
  rock shaped like your wife's oval

face, her neck; how her hair
    spreads long behind her, the wife in Paris,
  the wife who'd placed

the wire stating your death
        into a drawer, then onto a dress
    fitting, the sullen looking

woman who posed hours,
        days, months, as if to say *and how long
    will this take? Passage*

the critics said, the canvas
        breathing between three skulls on a table,
    where solids penetrate

each other, yet remain
        separate and safe. In your studio,
    when the guard turned away,

I fingered your pipe, spread
        your mother's black fan, wiped your wide comb's
    crooked teeth. Unchain my heart,

Mt. Ste. Victoire, I want
        my bond with flesh paid in sweat and yellow
    stamens, my garden trampled,

wholly blessed. Not to die
        before a rocky mountain face launching
    millions of tourist postcards

one can buy anyplace.

    I want my love's face before me, his sky-
vast blue-green eyes, and beyond,

unceasing clouds adrift,
    my fingertips on the slight lips I've kissed
so many times, I call mine.

Background Music

based on a line from "The Swan" by Marina Rainier Rilke, 1907

It's only when she shuts it off,
and hears the mantel clock's ticking,

she realizes he's no longer
in the air, for skimming books or

dusting shelves, not hearing, or half-
hearing to be fair, a distant

station, barely aware of a presence
abeyant, b-rated, for matter-of-

never fully being there, like
the low humming of a neighbor's

lawnmower, the music of her
narrow sphere. But take it away

and she's scared. What can she do?
Alone, she feels bereft, *I do,*

she'd said, *until death,* not knowing
parallel lives like swans floating

on glossy surfaces never
meet. *A swan laboring through*

what is still undone, but now it occurs
to her, one

will be left adrift.

The Prayer of the Bone

of the bone on the beach
      is to lie exposed, gleaning
  the moon's baldest vision,

and listen to the waves'
      ullagone, and not be moved.
  The prayer of the bone

is to veer like a gull,
     caught on a sudden updraft,
  disappear in the wind's

currents, to tug long
     and hard at the ocean's wide
  skirt, beg enfoldment.

Not to death, the bone prays,
     but to the movement between
  rolling waves, returning

to slide up the longing
     beach waiting for cover
  and comfort, to see sun

pour its guardian light
    next day over all it seeks,
  bringing life to the deep

waters, to the sleep of
     husbands and wives, hopeful for
  its kind keep, as they wake

to another morning's
    tasks, silently longing to know
the silent other, a strange

elbow in the air. Past
    years of her calling, "Who's there?"
  she hears only the sea's

tossing, and hurling wind,
      rain, yearning to be swept
  into the bone's prayer,

the movement between waves,
      the days and years, the buoy's
  foghorn, clasped by her ear.

The Odalisque

To see the light
outside the open
window the way

the brushstrokes
of the red sail-
boats and the pink

water pulsate
like the strings
of his violin, but

first: the balcony—
potted plants throb
against wilting

iron arabesques,
dissolve into specks—
as if the heat burns

his head and fogs
his panting spectacles—
and so the odalisque

steams with her
arms crossed above
her head, afraid

to wipe the pearling
sweat rolling down
her rippled nakedness

to the red river
of her pantaloons.
Amid the heavy

tapestries, black
lacquered screens,
Persian rugs, she

screams, "Mon Dieu!"
Matisse curses, not
seeing her, but the

pattern coming
apart

Amsterdam

The red tulip in the jam jar
on the café table

between our customary silence

lit ip the sunlit day
more than the Keukenhof

with its seven million

flowering bulbs.

Section II

Bygones

Time presses
The fire out
Leaves drop
In plots
Polar vortex
Chills the country
In late April
Daffodils sprout and wither
The birdfeeder emptied
The planted birdbath freed
Of purple promise
And white violets
Snow is heavy in Michigan
Heat scorches the Midwest
The crusted lake cracks
A wild red-throated turkey
Spreads
Beneath my window
And stares
A stone angel
Sits on the patio wall
Puts its hands
Between its legs
Tree limbs trimmed
Bare
A male cardinal alights
A branch
Why do you take so long
To come?
Two mallards meet and separate
Overnight came the summer
We didn't see spring

Van Gogh's Prayer

after Wheatfields with Crows, 1890

Let the crows fly from my heart,
dreams of destruction, exclusion, dreams
of inevitability, fantasies of power
and unreason. They feed of fear
and the feed of the desire
for a certainty, a frame, a skeleton
that fixes all things in the world.
The crows co-exist with heaven, hovering
around me a lifetime, harbingers
of gloom and death. Their eyes are black
as their feathers, bright black.
They fly over sickled wheat fields
with roads going nowhere.
Of the three roads I have painted,
give me the one that leads to the sky
where I have stood unstintingly,
whence comes the peace I find
when I am working. Let the dark blue
heaven have the crows, at once
my relief and resurrection.

From life, no road affords me peace,
only pain, the pain and the search
for peace. Loneliness was my creed
except for my brother, Theo, in whose arms
I shall die. So close, his belief in me. Yes,
I wanted people, turning myself
like a windmill gone haywire, cutting
my ear, swallowing paint, drinking absinthe.

Leave my heart, black crows,
let me be free, or are they coming,
their cawing calls, to rescue me?

The Glass House

Looking through the doors
See the many reflections
Mirrors of ourselves

Sun lights the bedrooms
We say goodbye to the moon
Soon shadowy palms

Awaken. Days sweep
Like swallows. Dusk floods the house.
Nothing to see through.

Late Inamorato

Swimming laps I no longer count, my still
honed body an arrow arcing back

to the quiver of life alone, I think of
what Flaubert wrote after first swimming

in the Red Sea—the caress of a thousand
liquid breasts—and face the skylights' bracing

flood, float clear of the sun, but before
a next stroke, bask in this onrushing ardor.

Thorns

His sometimes graceless movements gliding
into grace, hurrying, bent over to set down
a scalding Japanese tea cup on a granite slab
in the drizzle, the silence in his searching
eye under a twittering closed eyelid, and suddenly
his unswervingly looking up for the sound
of leaves, goldfinches, rain, or holding up low
thorny branches for her to pass, his slender hips
barely holding up washed thin jeans, his naked
back creased from a corroded iron bench
where they sat, wide-eyed, relaxed, but waiting,
not saying what hung in the air—a row of navy
briefs, six blue long sleeved shirts—all that rush
inside them, the falls nearby, white foam and roar,
his sitting in a plastic white chaise and her
in a hard mud splattered green lawn chair,
her coming over brushing his thighs and shins,
always covered in long pants as he ran, no
never ran, but ambled the trails of his own
making to the river, where she kept coming back
to his back, trying to enter the impenetrability
of his vast domain, having no room for her.

You Drew a Blank

When the muse leaves, she goes
through the front door, drops
her key on the tabletop,

takes her traveling laptop,
keeping your desktop
closed and neat, next to her coffee

mug. She admires
your steadfastness, but, of course,
wants more, for you

to leave myths of goddesses
behind the everyday
world and for you to spread outdoors.

She critiques (incommunicably)
your attempts and writes
continual clichés

to replace your work. Admit
you like your own work;
her poems are a bore.

There's a blank in your heart
where bank tellers
were before, giving out

large bills, no signature
required. The dollars spread like pelicans
over the shore, whatever

they fetched you felt surely
there'd be more. Then
you wrote feverishly:

you loved the way she adored
holding your coffee, the best
she ever tasted.

Bite My Ear Tango

The body gets lonely two
legs want yours entwined

wants a breast to nest
and nipple speak

a navel to press
the button to the upper

terrace where I loved
your shoulders just for

supporting your neck
and head as my Blaze roses

climbed your trellis best
Miracle-gro stems bringing out

the brightest in each other
like the crimson amaryllis

I bought you
its large puckering lips

are they still trumpeting
without me?

Constable's Sorrow

after Constable's Seascape Study With Rain Clouds, 1827

I would weep for him, were I not still
such an unfeeling Englishman. Sitting
with him on a shingle beach at Orford Ness,
saying nothing for hours, and yet confessing
my shingle hearted flintiness, breathing in
the unfailing salt sea-smell, the broken seaweed
and the shipwrecked stars and the stoniness
of the wind that has leveled the land, making it
the exact equal of the sea. His wife,
Maria, soon to be dead, his *skeying*
days, soon to be over, and all that
is left unsaid when a beloved wife
dies, his and mine.

Never am I completely
at home by the sea, although a hint of that
exists by the water, but not where
the sand's cut away, leaving a little cliff
that happens often by the sea. The water
cuts away and cuts away at the same line,
the tides not sliding over the beach,
always these signs of depredations,
leaving me beleaguered, overlain
by threats and danger, a feeling as old
to me as all my memories. A year,
my dark solitude spread on the ground—
his unfurled funereal clouds overhead.

A Gone World

The orchid opened
completely.
I'll have a friend care for it
while I'm gone.
Did you leave Saturday?
I left it open
for you.
But you were gone.

The flower I bought for you. Orchis
drank too much,
tried to rape a priestess
of Dionysus.
The Bacchanalian tore him apart.
The gods

changed him.
into a flower.
His name, from the shape
of the root,
meaning testicle.

I put up my hair
slowly.
I found a sign that
you'd been here
in the mirror—
the orchid.
It leans toward
the window,
opens like a mouth.

Stepping once more
onto a plane. Come
track me down,
trace my scent. Let
the orchid be your guide.

The Necklace

The stone stands its ground,
Worn away turning
in the whirls of surf,
chuffed to the beach, sun-
      drenched, rain-washed,
a map of injuries.

The pearl grows from an itch,
      a pinch, which becomes
      itself.
Pearls are like planets, circling
      the sky, our wish for
      something unbroken:
beyond the ashen glow of the dark moon.

The pearl, the drama of forgetting.
The stone, the trauma of remembering.

Bonnard's Wife's Ashes

Stooped shoulders, small breasts. The womanly
head bent, Marthe, the model
he made wife in 1925,

She was upset someone might whisper, "She's one
of those women, one doesn't
marry." Even here,

her meager shoulders seem to carry
lead. The shadow of her head
blackens the tub.

She invented a life, assumed a name, de Meligny,
this demimondaine, daughter
of a carpenter, said her family

was dead. She was always taking baths, obsessed
with water. Marthe walked like a bird
on tiptoe, the weightless walk

that comes from wings. Raspy voice, strict diets
She ordered raw meat in restaurants,
saw no one but her husband.

The doctors couldn't figure what ailed her.

Though in 384 paintings, she was young, full
fleshed. And when she died
at 72, he locked the door

to her room, finished the last tub painting:
four years rearranging,
decomposing, ending

                their long estrangement, his painting,
                        her bathing.

No wonder all the baths; she needed

to feel weightless, as

he drowned her in light.

A Red Dachshund

after Pierre Bonnard's The Bathroom, 1932

I never saw mauve
before Bonnard's nude
in the bathroom. How
could a body be so purple
and warm? She reflects
everything, stepping
into an orange basin
with her shoes on. Here,
where color makes no sense
but to itself, why should anything else?
The orange curtain behind her,
the seated red dachshund
on a white reflection below her,
the blue and orange
lozenge tiles on either side
of her, the shocking pink
of her dressing gown, falling
from a shelf, sing out
in rounds. I am lost, looking down
or across, perspective thrown off
by a glut of color. She picks up
the pink, the red, orange
and blue, and strikes
mauve precisely at five
on the clock face, fixing
the white splash
on her breast, the sun
streaming in
through the slats.

Discards

after the paintings of Giorgio Morandi (1890-1964)

the detachment of objects
when the sea is swept out of them
from a submerged shore
the unearthed treasure
of a wide lipped metal pitcher
brushed matte

        oyster-white

a caffè latte bowl
a blue fluted egg cup
given their washed yellow souls
he afforded tossed or lost objects
his name centered above

like skywriting
"Morandi"
all his life living
with three sisters and mother
steering through their rooms
to his own secrets
of hiding and cropping
misperceiving and bleeding
color into dullness and neutrality
a thing making itself alive

The Handkerchief

Oh, Othello, you say the handkerchief
      is too small for your breaking head. It grows
larger in the play every moment.
      Oh, Desdemona, how could you let
the handkerchief fall? Oh, Emilia, how could you
      give the handkerchief to your heinous husband?
What could you take from me? What talisman?
      Nothing so exotic as a handkerchief
woven by a magical seamstress: as long
      as Othello's mother kept it, his father's love
was safe. Is there any item in my plentiful
      wardrobe that accrues such magic that would
enrage my husband, if I lost it?
      He wears the same ring of 51 years. I've lost
four wedding rings which piqued him, my carelessness,
      his heart, and every time I look at his plain gold
ring, I am pained that I don't have mine.
      What has he given me that if lost
would hold the weight of the handkerchief?
      The white gold necklace he bought for me
in Greece? Oh, lustrous necklace, neither proof
      of chastity nor magic, I wish
I had nothing, never so dear to lose
      as that handkerchief, its strawberries,
the emblem of the hymen broken, embroidered
      on the white of chastity. I lose scarves
in cars, in movie theaters, in the wind. To hold
      something so dearly meant to the giver,
I couldn't be trusted. Oh, darling husband, what
      you have to give to me is not found
in the material world, but I am thinking hard

upon it. What you have given me
is the honor every day of being your wife.
So a little boredom crawls in. Your shouting
from the kitchen, "You know I can't hear you in here!"
"Come *downstairs*." "The refrigerator is empty."

Section III

When the Light Changed

waking in bed, my arms widespread
      against the light
as right as a sparrow's wing
      on my heart
after we make love, the covers pulled over
my breasts, and then

running headlong to the sunroom,
      the grasp of the sea
close and eager, the sun
      a Monet
painting, his rushing out at daybreak planting
paints and easel,

seeing the soul of his fixed eye,
      above the new
horizon, a beach ball throwing
      a pearly
orange ladder across the sea, and only then
he began to draw

each day's truth, "a puddle of clothes
on the ground," you saw, not seeing
it was your wife. I'd run ahead
to the street, excited by the bristling
Gallic step dancers.

I am always running ahead, perhaps
for the last time,—*struck head-on by a car while crossing the*
street,
then
thrown 20-30 feet, coma scale about 5. She is combative. There is
a hematoma
of the right anterior occiput.

for the last time
    looking for a belt,

                            a shoe—for hours
              sleeping every afternoon
              watching *Sex & The City*
                      anytime it was on

*on physical examination she would moan but would not answer
questions or follow commands*

"you had a great party"

*Patient pulled dressing off bilateral knee wounds sitting at end of
bed yelling, "I need to get out of here, I'll do better at home."
Turning from side to side complaining of feeling tired continues to
ask the same question, "Where's my Lego?"*

*"I want to go home. I don't want to stay here another minute." She
keeps asking
for her husband. Morphine for pain and knee lacerations, still
restless.*

turning on the escalator
      looking up to say
I love you—each time I fall
dashing ahead
you're there how
can I understand

                   *Remains disoriented. She will be impulsive and
irrational.*

Purchasing Dolce & Gabanna sunglasses
        wanting to look like Sophia Loren
Wanting to wear a tight white sequined tank top
Wanting Marcello to me rescue me from the Trevi Fountain
Hearing my name: the subdural bleed unabsorbed
        a month later
Outside the building leaning
     against a hot brick wall
     after another MRI
Crying not knowing why

Debbie's calling from Palm Desert, "why didn't you tell me?"
        "I didn't want to ruin your vacation"
sleeping all afternoon
walking with Larry, a Dante scholar
        from Milwaukee, wanting him
        to salve my burning knees
first reading in the Eagle Eye Book Store
sitting at the table, a nearby restaurant,
        a margarita party which Angel threw, what a turnout!
saying I want to go home
        meaning leaving Atlanta for Milwaukee

Personal History: She is married. She is a poet.
Thinking! Sylvia Plath wouldn't like that.
I remember thinking.

Life's Not a Novel

"Let sleeping dogs lie," you say
rolling over when I tell you
Molly and Leopold Bloom slept
head to tail end, stopped
having sex.

What is it like to walk away
from the stove, not worry about
weather in Morocco? To sleep
in Van Gogh's wheat fields
or float on Rothko's islands?
What is the trick? Is it too late
to learn? Do you dare disturb
the Universe? I want to.

I sit back in an elephantine
chair from an Edith Wharton
novel and dwell on Lily Bart's
choices. Mine are not so awful.

"Life's not a novel or a picture
by Picasso," you repeat once
too often in an ear I cut off,
send along to your office.

So I Go Shopping

the car won't start
the sky is dark
I left my purse in the park
my printer's jammed
I hurt my hand
hammering it

I lost three wedding bands
but not the husband
breakneck me
struck by a car
flung afar
my head soon shaved

like the burning monks
my mind blown back
to the photo of Kim Phuc
her napalmed arms
at 25 I was a mother

at Ft. Bliss shopping
for sequined tops
chain belts
heavy metal handbags
camouflage

on the streets of Juarez
little boys selling cigarettes
all night long
whores not filmed
in *The World of Suzie Wong*
I eat cheap filet mignon
drink tequila and orange
so I go shopping

years later
at a Miami mall
mothers pushing strollers
at a clip
and my parent roping
arms and I'm angry
at my husband
for not buying
long term health
insurance

so I shopping
for a $1000 vintage
nude photograph
and he doesn't see
why her thigh
is a reminder

of the beauty
of the parts
not being bigger
than the whole
we never got
so I go shopping

when I should
thank god
he didn't have to go to,
undergo Viet Nam
what hell I undertook

in that desert hole
called El Paso
where I got my fix

at Ft. Bliss
lost my soul
to Benzedrine and scotch
so I go shopping

for the honey and the love
for the baby I cut out
of a future
family book
for an end that never took

Auguries from the Writer's Colony

Careening gulls clamor like star-crossed lovers outside the window. I hide behind closed patio doors in a cheap Florida hotel where residing plastic flamingos convene on the lawn like little Lolitas. Did Leda close her eyes, or were they wild and terrified? Someone is feeding the gulls from above. Their cries burst like pomegranate seeds in Persephone's mouth, who swallows the new taste and decides it can't be all bad on the dark side.

Pounding, canted wings close in, slaphappy sleeves on a line. I'd sew shirts out of nettles if they were my brothers doing time, but I'm not a princess. The gulls' shrieks tear at my liver. Whose lines did I steal this time? I pull the curtains back a little and see them spiraling like Dante's *terza rima*. I'm afraid they'll pluck out my eyes. They did it to Cinderella's stepsisters. Pretending the shoe fit, they were ridiculous.

I want to dive with the gulls and not come up a suicide, like Magritte's drowned mother, her nightgown pulled over her head. She'd never see him paint a woman's face using her genitals, *The Rape*. I pull gray tissue paper over the bay, like a haze bred from Monet's steadfast gaze. I'm afraid to look at an empty sky. I'm afraid there's nothing good I can come up with—that's mine.

Worry Doll

READ ALL DIRECTIONS CAREFULLY BEFORE BEGINNING

Take 1 clothespin, 2
toothpicks, tacky glue,
4 yards of floss, and a mother

standing over you who says
it looks like rain
when the sky's perfectly

blue. On that
cue, place a dab of glue
on the back of neck to secure

floss and wrap it tightly
around the upper
body. So what if your breasts

languish from lack of air. Cover
the clothespin completely,
no one must guess from what

cloth you're cut. To cut
your losses early, don't try
to remember your hands

are tied. As for the face,
use black magic
marker: dots for eyes,

and since you're not fully
realized, skip the nose,
an upside down crescent

mouth for spilling no
onto everything. Add a bow
or not. This will be the gloss

of your tearful childhood,
full of woes and bad
people, trust only your own

kind. Wrap and secure
the doll five or six times.
Then start over.

"Mirror, Mirror On The Wall"

                           Startling,
my brows are disappearing like leaves
outside my late autumn window, leaving me

a new sea view. Will I see better without
those architectural guides, showing

consternation, fear, joy, surprise? Without
pencil and liquid dispenser, what could I depend on?

A bit of cover-up smooths, soothes the forehead,
softens the fuller nose. Blush, powder, lipstick,

I dab on; if this is ripeness, and "all"
I don't want it. "Get used to it," a friend says.

Used to it? Powder, hardly ever. I remember
my mother's caked compacts, I opened

and closed to see myself in the mirrors.
Foundation, I think of the undergarments

she wore: tight, encompassing, I leave off.
They seem to fill every crevice, pronouncing

them deeper more. Concealer, I use on the spots
rising like chicken pocks. Bronzer? I used to lie

on the beach sun tan oiled; I'm out of skin stock.
Yes, I say to even tone matte. Who doesn't

want to look even toned? Who stayed, who left,
who lived, who died? The years go by, but I don't?

Yes, give me the dewy glow, the contours
of twenty years ago, the high cheek bones,

chiseled chin, slender upturned nose, the high
forehead. "Do you want a makeover?" I'm asked.

The spark in the large dark brown eyes remains.
I leave the counter unsurrendering,

but for $50 in supplies.

Givenchy Lavender

Body my house…
—May Swenson

mother not interred
in my silk lavender
dress but in the 10
pieces of linen prescribed
by faith a mistake
my younger brother
kept secret for a year
afraid to return it
or the satin shoes I'd laid out
for her passage
her shameful body
not to show through
to the crowd
my childish fear
concealed until now
recalling how she'd let
herself go all to hell
yelling she'd go to the poorhouse
on my account
mark my words
and don't you forget it
then a slap across the mouth

The Chicken

Goose bumped and stretched, a row of scrawny necks dangles in the window like a curtain to a horror show. A chicken for each pot in twenty blocks, nails in them and whatnot. Dad got caught in the black market, made front page when I was in the incubator.

Mother is the chicken lady, big breasted and fat. I dream of her in a white apron, a trussed chicken everyone grabs. She burns their pin feathers and laughs. Crossing streets, she grabs me by the neck; I won't hold hands that stink of chicken fat.

The wings and the dark greasy legs part easily from the carcass, torn apart like my Tiny Tears doll when I get mad. I take the wishbone, put my thumb on top, but my younger brother beats me. Bones picked clean as black marbles, the hollow of the animal, collapsed. I go out on the street with my pea shooter. Target practice at pigeons.

Moon over Francesca's

how it almost touched the turret
of the large Tudor house across
the street where it shone Buddha-like

above an ominous maple—
black as my labyrinthine dreams
all that first week in the new house

darkly lit, like the long tunnels
I ran through in Steel Pier's fun house,
peed my pants there, scared from the howls

I heard ahead, scared of dancing
skeletons overhead, and I
kept on running until I reached

a hall of mirrors turning me
pencil thin or fat as a cow—
Borden's Elsie who says, *don't*

look now, but it's my black and white
head spiked on a double wrought iron
hook in your father's meat market,

and it's her moon eyes finding me
behind a cold case of yellow
gizzards, maroon calves' livers, brick-

red hamburger, my Crayola
boxed colors, my father so mean
to my mother—I could murder—
why does everything come back raw?

Portrait

Her arms around me—child—
              —George Oppen

Her arm around me, around my waist,
          holding her bare arm around me
As if I would fall off the map of her plaid soft lap,
The sad look in her eyes bore into my own—the sad look
          and my peevish brother, and my
                    hands pressed,
Tightly into my wool skirt, its waistband itchy.

It is the girl who falls from her—
the brother is the honorable branch,
separate in the photograph, inconsolable
in his tweed suit and knit vest,
nothing to give her.

Aphrodite at South Beach

I saw in you the robust beauty
of a woman "a certain age"—gold bangle

bracelets, necklace, hoop earrings, a lime
bikini with a hot pink hibiscus

covering each buoyant breast. Standing
at the water's scalloped edge, you were about

to wade in. Your bronze thighs and buttocks, weathered
and dimpling, had yet a staunch strength in them—

like an old dulcimer. Your bracelets jingled.
Your earrings shimmered. Sunglasses hid your eyes,

the sea-sparkle that blinded Paris. And then,
Aphrodite, "lover of laughter," I heard your peals

of gold like coins clinking in a purse. How
many have tried to re-invent your magic

girdle? An older man, bearded Poseidon,
was calling you to come in, *venez, venez,*

waving his arms like hairy tridents.
Daughter of the seasperm wave, body

surfer of horses' white manes, I saw you
dive, come up, without your weighty chains.

Wet at the Shallows

Blue branched veins leaping
Out of crunched hands dripping sand
For ornate castles

Wet at the shallows
where mothers sat on beach chairs
every Saturday

With their brown paper
bags (Acme) of plums, peaches,
to fill our hunger

Freckled, feckless life-
Guards on high stands calling us
As sandbars shifted

Lest we were stranded
Swimming our sand crab crawls
To get to the shore

Ice cream men with ice
Boxes slung across their backs
"Give your tongue a ride!"

To scamper the boards
The sun each day announcing
A new beginning

To endless summer
Who saw the shortest distance
Is an arc between

Two points? We soar, fall,
by late afternoon. We end
at the wooden pier's

long shored up pilings.

Section IV

Quick Lessons in Simplified Drawings

You slipped off like a sleeve on a sweater
            unraveling.
I shiver from your cold.
You blow your nose.
Motion don't come near;
I don't want you to catch it.

I can't catch anything.
You're in the Urals.
The trans-Siberian railway labors
        between two place settings,
our switching seats like musical chairs,
            going from touch to naught.
A cut-off composition—like a sleeve.
The paper sleeve for fish wrap.
That's how the impressionists learned
            from the Japanese.
Background scaled down.
Angles sharply cut
            what's unnecessary.
For you or for me?

Hokusai's cranes are all foreground.
Thought to mate for life.
They dance and call.
Males joyously jumping
        over the female.

What can I wrap?
What will I sing?
Who will dance over me?

There Are Rooms

in my house I visit only
in dreams, doors that spring wide open
   down connecting halls as I raise
my gloved hand to close them, inside
   English country houses, paisley
couches, and sheer curtains tousled

   gently inward, the spare light
filling clear glass pitchers. Scarlet
   and purple peonies blaze, a desk's
Tiffany vase, more in a quilted
   spread where time folds like a napkin:
at breakfast, I'm still buttering

   your toast, layering black current
jam with a loving hand. In one
   room I rest under a four poster's
midnight blue starred canopy,
   counting the children promised
to Abraham. I do not think

   I am one of them. A large room
at the Inn, a chest of drawers
   in charcoal shadow, a bed against
the wall, a porch ahead, where I glimpse
   steeples, shallow clouds, and beyond—
white cold Vermont hills. With you,

   I thought there was no end, and now
naked and restless under this stiff
   sheet, I hear the keys to other rooms,
rustling brocades, cries of love,
   keys turning in me all afternoon,
never to turn for us again.

The Sound of Grass

Let it arrive at my feet
       like a quick falling leaf
    in the first barely

perceived autumn breeze,
       or a favorite aunt's last kiss
    on the forehead

or a silk sleeve forming
       gently as a tear on a child's flushed
    cheek. Where's her lost

catcher's mitt? And will she find it
       before the game? Let it come
    in deep sleep

like the sound of grass sprouting
       in the front yard or even
    like the S.U.V.

that plowed me down, crossing
       the street. Let death come
    unerringly and clean.

Losing

losing a glove I'd shoved
in my pocket, worn supple

and dull, the red lining
torn, the signature

prescription glasses, gold wire
circles set inside squares, left

between the glass salt and pepper
shakers on the bistro's table

the night before Mikaela left
for college. A scarf adrift

in a cab, silk-screened sea-green—
Atlantic City's ocean before

the tide of hospital wastes
washed ashore. After school,

I'd watch TV until the car
pulled into the drive, knowing

I'd survived. But since you died,
Mom, each loss carves a deeper

hollow. Waiting for you
to come home from our bloody

butcher shop, carrying
the wax-papered wrapped meat,

how we ate, how we thrived. How
the blood flowed into our lives.

Egypt

I went on a trip and lost an alphabet,
learning to read a bird or a feather
along the Nile that carried the basket

with Moses bound in a Levite blanket,
his mother becoming the muddy river,
her murmurs also a lost alphabet

in the bulrushes where Miriam let
down the pitch covered cradle, watching over
her brother along the Nile, the basket

moving beside our boat at sunset.
On deck I let silence like a sweater
wrap me; I felt I'd lost an alphabet.

Caught in the past like a fish in a net,
seeing death everywhere with no sister
or seer to follow a homely basket

drifting down the darkening river, sweat
dripping down from my armpits, the closer
I come to a mother's lost alphabet
along the Nile that once carried the basket.

No More Arguments

Their heads have long been lost, as have their hands,...
—B. F. Cook, The Elgin Marbles

Good news, Persephone hopes,
stuck in a frieze, out of sync
with her own story, signifying
everything about mothers
and daughters, after
the dark parts.

Demeter puts her arm
on her daughter's turned
shoulder, but Persephone's
greeting Artemis, who's looking
for her cape, the purple one
that used to sail behind her.

Demeter's lips are pursed.
The young women laugh.
Picking flowers in a field,
Persephone felt the earth yield.
Hades gave her fruit
no mother could.

A hefty foot emerges
from the drapery—
Demeter's—they wear the same
clothes now, two female figures,
carved from a single block.

No more arguments.
Springtime and the daughter's
home. She wants to see her friends—
like this one rushing
toward her—.

They want all the news
of hell.

Wading

"What happened,"
says little Sophie, now
diapered with sand, water

dribbling from her sippie
cup into deeper water,
the waves up to her waist

and the sun disappearing
fast. Her mother holds out
a towel, once blue as the morning

horizon. Indeed, what happened
to the arcing sunsets, hula
girl palms, sequined tights

of beach, tide pooled
piazzas? The indelible
Kodak honeymoons, undated

black and whites in peeling
leather albums, shoved
in a bureau drawer. Sepia

bubbe and zayde, finger-
waved aunts, stooped
mustached uncles, one

who pinched my thigh under
the table, then laughed
Atlantic City photos of Mom

and Dad in rolling chairs, (later
wheelchairs in Miami), brothers
and me as babies, my

offspring. Almost daily,
digitals arrive of the latest
grandchild like this one,

knee-deep in pounding
tides, that quizzical look
I'd recognize anywhere.

"Get up, Sophie, girl, scoop
the years like sand
in your pink fists, years

light as pinfeathers, the ones
your great-grandmother, after
5,000 miles of steerage, singed

from thousands of chickens,
providing the mother mulch
for your survival and mine by

selling chickens in a butcher
shop, cooking, cleaning, taking
care, leaving bitter tears

to the ocean." "Come, Sophie,
take my hand, and we'll put
the photos in the albums, dry-eyed."

Mise en Scène

A small window lets the light
into an alcove off a boudoir.
The bed is empty.

A white porcelain tub with claw
feet and a pedestal sink
ripen to pink.

Flickering leaves cast
shifting shadows
on the faded floral wall-

paper. For formal drapery,
a towel tossed over
a piano stool.

Steam rolls over
a mirror, screening
broad buttocks rising

from the deep
tub. A few wet tendrils
fall from an upswept

hairdo—loose ends
to wrap up
the painting of

The Bather, the full-
sized woman, celebrated
by artists

who knew how to draw
a curtain
call each time

a body called.
My own standing
form ripples

in the splashing
sunlight from
outside the window

to the sun porch
overlooking the rugged
bluff to the ocean.

The waves call, and fall
all night, through the bough-
laden trees, waiting

for me to take part
in the production,
no lines, no rehearsal.

The Girl in the Stone Creek Coffee Shop

after Ezra Pound

The girl in the Stone Creek Coffee Shop
Is as beautiful as ever.
The August heat has not frazzled her.
She makes the caffés lattés eagerly;
    Though she will also turn middle-aged.
      And the bubble of her youth she blows before us
    As she puts down our cups
      Will not enclose us when the foam settles.

Olympia

I have seen elephants cradle the skulls
of dead bulls in their trunks, hurl them,
try to crush them into the ground, pace
a few steps, turn back, smell them again
before moving on with the journey.

I step carefully over broken columns,
fallen friezes, florid capitals rooted
in the ground like decapitated heads.
I wrap my arms around one. I must go
to the museum to see the head of Hera.

Water From a Rock

The dove coos in Mary's ear, fluttering
      its wings against her moist cheek as she sleeps

on a courtyard bench. Flying up, the dove drops
      its feathers. Mary awakens haloed.

"All my life I cook meals for tables of hungry
      men. It is like giving birth to feathers

that keep changing into earthly shapes.
      What did the spirit say to move me?

'Give them away.' Then my appetites slept
      in a grave. The blue mantle covered me.

They came by the thousands to worship me
      on a high gilded throne. Later, they came

only to feast. Up from the ducklings and squabs,
      and roast legs of lamb, their febrile eyes

scorched mine, draining the pools to the bottom.
      Soon I felt worthless. I smiled and tried to look

merciful. The weight of the mantle pressed me
      like an olive. Where are the miracles:

a burning bush, a sun stayed, water
      from a rock? Ever since that long night

in the stable, I long to slip off the mantle,
      put my feet into sandals, into earth."

As He Painted

after Pierre Bonnard's Siesta, 1900

who knows maybe she slept
maybe he never said
    a prayer
    she wouldn't
    move
color was what he knew
while Marthe lay there
the wallpaper of every
      hotel room the same
    to her
where he tacked the canvas
    to the wall

as he painted
the curve of her back
      shadowed
the oil lamp yellowing
      her buttocks
her naked foot atop
      her other leg
her arms under
      the pillow
the slight breast on the bed
her hands under her head
the dog Pouce attending her

as he painted
      the day grew hotter
      the covers wilting
like green cabbage
      he remembers
to give the dog water
      how hard it is

to catch the color
how easy it is
for Marthe to lie
in her own space,
languidly.

Athens Intercontinental

Outside my window in a blue-gray haze,
the Parthenon, swathed like a Christo
monument, stands forsaken. Across
the way a blue glass bowling alley reflects
the sun's smog sheathed blades, its tubular
staircase whirling into space. To the left,
big black block letters strike **Continental.**
To the right, **BMW, Panasonic.** Where's Athena,
her aegis of Medusa, those deathless snakes?

I close and open the curtain on a Greek
bride heaving under pregnant tiers of dust.
Shell and battered gutted like a rainbow
trout, she reminds faithful to herself. No one
walks between her massive pillars, imbibes
her cool and calm resolve resides in her
watering shade, breathes in her perfect
calculations. She is the shell of memory,
the bank where I deposit my grain.

Unorthodox rows of box-white houses,
like excavated molars, rot the landscape.
Laundry hangs as it always has, empty
and waiting. A few cypresses take me upward.
The Acropolis is closed. A strike, the hotel
bellhop explains, rubbing his ochre stained
thumb and forefinger. I give him his tip:
400 drachmas. Strike up the band.
Tomorrow I leave for the islands

Mattisse in Morocco

(1)

A silent gate is peeling.
A pelican hook on a swag chain yawns.
The morning is halfway
open like the market stalls.
I listen to an ostrich
going down a stairway
to the beach.
From an Arab café
overlooking the harbor,
I walk down any slanting alley
into fluid blue shadows
and lose my way.

(2)

The men play cards, gamble,
watch a goldfish bowl,
a vase of red flowers.
Their blank faces tell me
they have succumbed
to hashish.
So what do I do?

I have my goldfish
bowl and my pink flower.
I want my flower pink, otherwise
it's not my flower anymore.
Unlike the fish which could be yellow,
so yellow is what they'll be.

(3)

For two weeks, deluge.
I write to Gertrude Stein,
"Why did I come?" "The light
is superb, the weather too variable."
The rain fades. Astride a donkey,
I cross the countryside,
but not before breathing in
the red lining of my model's
slippers, the goldfish,
the gardens. Illumined,
I see nothing but the light.

As We Say Goodbye

Your warm body in the cold sea, warm
        a shivering me. I dive between your legs, circle
  your slender girth, grasp your smooth shoulders,
   all the tender width of you, as if
       I were as supple as shoaling minnows.

Afterward, scampering over stones, pebbles, sand,
        beside the insistent roar of the water, drowning
 our constant conversation, you bounce the beach's
       currency into the water, two, three times.
           They skim the waves, the rising levels,

are not tides, you say, filling me with joy
       at your side. How did it come to be this way?
The sharpness of your narrow blue eyes
      lead you to creatures unknown to me.
        Your steadily thinning hair, reveal a startling

naked self, pushing onward, never slacking, pushing beyond
       your limits, or to the limit of all
you entail. A mortal who must face the dying day
     as we say goodbye to all that is fluid,
        to the end of this sequined salted sea.

Golden Autumn

after Monet's Impression, Sunrise (1873)

Each morning, when the sun streams into
the bedroom from the lake, I think of
Monet's *Impression, Sunrise,* how he did it
in one sitting. No, he was standing
at a window overlooking the harbor
at Le Havre to catch the light. Three boats,
almost black, derricks, cranes, anchored ships,
an orange and pink sky fill the painting.
A ladder of light slips past the boats, not quite
reaching the shore. When he moved to Giverny
he had a gardener clear all the plants
and flowers that were dead or dying
before he awoke, to trim one's life to what
is alive, when we are all dying.
Plein air painting, he sought, consumed, abounded.
I wake to the light, the golden leaves
of autumn bustling on the bluff leading
to the lake. Hardly, anyone speaks of his
jumping into the Seine trying to kill
himself, distraught with his apparent
failure of painting, acclaiming a new way
of looking at light, coming in through
my blinds, the pink sky over the horizon
filling me with beauty and hope. The leaves
are fast falling. This is my golden autumn.
The two of us here under the covers
and I know we have another day of light.
To see the light, one has to see the dark.

About the Author

Paula Goldman's book, *The Great Canopy,* won the Gival Press Poetry award and received an honorable mention for the Independent Booksellers' Award. Her work has appeared in *Oyez Review, Slant, Calyx, Passager, Ekphrasis, Rattle, Prairie Schooner, Manhattanville Review, Cream City Review, Comstock Review, Harvard Review, The North American Review, Poet Lore, Poet Miscellany, Hawaii Pacific Review, Cæsura,* and other magazines. Her poems have appeared in *Boomer Girls* published by the University of Iowa Press, *The Party Train: A Collection of North American Prose Poetry* published by New Rivers Press and most recently, *Conversation Pieces* published by Knopf. She was the first prize winner in **INKWELL's** (Manhattanville College) poetry competition and the Louisiana Literature Award for poetry. She holds an MA degree in Journalism from Marquette University and an MFA in Writing from Vermont College. A former reporter for *The Milwaukee Journal,* she served as a docent and lecturer at the Milwaukee Art Museum for twenty-five years. Her manuscript *Late Inamorato* was a finalist for the Gival Press Poetry Award. New poems have appeared in *Cæsura* and *Arlington Literary Journal.* Paula was nominated for a Pushcart Prize 2017. She lives in Milwaukee, Wisconsin, with her husband, Allan. They have been married fifty-three years, and have two grown children and three grandchildren.

www.ingramcontent.com/pod-product-compliance
Lightning Source LLC
Chambersburg PA
CBHW022013080426
42733CB00007B/582